MW01147654

Destiny & Courage

"For the Christian Life"

"Lessons on the Road to Maturity"

Written and Edited By

Pastor/Evangelist Chuck L. Turner Sr.

Cover Design By

The Prophet X Commons

Acknowledgements

I dedicate this book to my mother Florence Lee Turner, the strongest woman I know. Also to my beautiful wife LaVenise Young Turner who has stood by my side through thick and thin. Also my children Cyndal M. Turner, the one who makes my heart smile, Chuck L. Turner Jr., and Devon A. Turner. I would also like to thank Pastor Sonny and Sister Julie Arguinzoni the founders of Victory Outreach International, one of the greatest ministries in the world, for their love, kindness, and example throughout the years. Special thanks to Pastor/Elder David Martinez (R.I.P.) and Sister Faith Martinez my spiritual mom and dad without whose help I wouldn't be who I am today. Also thank you to Pastor Augie Barajas and Sister Mary Barajas for their influence in my life when I returned to California. Also thank you to my current Pastor Michael Gonzalez and his wife Sister Christina Gonzalez for not only encouraging me but allowing me to pursue what God has called me to do. And finally thank you to the many Pastors all over the world who have graciously allowed me the privilege of standing behind their pulpits to minister the word of God as I have treasured each and every opportunity!

Pastor/Evangelist Chuck L Turner Sr.

All scripture references are from the New King James Version of the bible.

Introduction

After growing up running the streets of
Altadena/Pasadena and becoming addicted
to crack cocaine, Pastor Chuck Turner gave
his life to the Lord in 1987 during his stay at
the Men's Recovery Home in Victory
Outreach of the San Fernando Valley. He
then served for 17 years under the direction
and leadership of Pastor/Elder David
Martinez. After attending Bible School
Pastor Chuck became a licensed minister
with Victory Outreach International in 1993
and served in the local church (VOSFV) as
an Associate Pastor, Marriage Counselor,
Worship Leader, Choir Director, Bible
School Instructor, and Recovery Home
Director. In 1999 after hearing the call of
God Pastor Chuck began ministering as an
Evangelist, singing and preaching in many
churches across the United States. There
was a challenge given to him in 2004 to take

over a small struggling church in Washington, DC and Pastor Chuck accepted. He then served from November 2004 through October 2012 as Senior Pastor of Victory Outreach Washington, DC. After sensing the leading of the Holy Spirit to return to the Evangelistic field he returned to California. From October 2012 until July 2015 he served as an International Evangelist with Victory Outreach Eagle Rock as his home church, under the leadership of Senior Pastor/International Prayer Leader Augie Barajas. While in Eagle Rock Pastor Chuck also lead a Bible Study for married couples. In August 2015 Pastor Chuck, along with his wife and daughter relocated to Palmdale, California and is presently serving as an Associate Pastor/International Evangelist with Victory Outreach Palmdale as his home church under the leadership of Pastor Michael Gonzalez. Pastor Chuck Turner has been with his wife LaVenise Turner for 40 years, (30 years married), they have three children, Cyndal Turner,

Chuck Turner Jr., and Devon Turner. Over the years he has sang and preached at many churches throughout the United States, also in Europe and New Zealand. Pastor Chuck has recorded three separate musical projects and been privileged to sing at many conferences and conventions, as well as acting and singing in several musical productions with Victory Outreach International. He was also granted the opportunity to speak at the Victory Outreach World Conference in 2005 at the Long Beach Convention Center. From the East Coast to the West Coast and many places in between as well as abroad, God has used his life to win souls and strengthen the saints for the work of the kingdom!

Preface

What does it take to become a mature Christian? I'm not sure anyone can give an answer that would fit every person striving for growth and personal development as a child of God. What I can do is talk about what it took for me to become a mature Christian with the confidence of knowing that it will be a help to many people who are open to what I have to say on this most important subject.

Let's face it the average believer is not on a relentless quest to grow in their walk with God. I use the word average and not the word normal because average deals with numbers or percentages if you will. So when I say average I'm talking about the greater majority in a given situation. On the other hand the word normal deals with expectation. So when I say a "normal believer" I'm thinking of someone who is living Christ-like because Jesus modeled the lifestyle we as believers are expected to emulate. Too many believers today behave as though doing what the scripture says earns them some extra credit when in fact it's simply the normal expectation for a Christian life. Jesus said in Luke 17:10, "So likewise you, when you have done all those things which you are commanded, say, 'We are unprofitable servants. We have done what was our duty to do.'"

  Sadly, the truth about the church today is that the average Christian doesn't pray regularly, read the word regularly, give regularly, love or forgive consistently, or serve in any capacity within the ministry. In other words they mostly just go to church. But a normal Christian does more than just go to church. The normal Christian is constantly on a mission to grow in their relationship with God. I'm happy to belong to a ministry like Victory Outreach International where the goal is to see every Christian come to maturity in their walk with the Lord and answer the calling God has for their life. So after thirty years of serving the Lord I've learned some lessons about growth and I'd like to pass them on. Have I got all together? Not by a long shot! But like the Apostle Paul says, "I press toward the goal for the prize of the upward call of God in Christ Jesus." Philippians 3:14.

Let's agree that it takes maturity to reach our **Destiny**, and it takes **Courage** to commit to a lifestyle of growth. With that being said I pray this book will inspire you moving forward and help you find the strength for the honest self-examination necessary for personal growth. So here it is, **Destiny & Courage "For the Christian Life"** I pray you're blessed by its content!

Chapter One
"A Lesson on Anger"

I suppose if there's one thing that we all have to learn to manage, it's our anger. There's no getting around it we all get angry and we all express it differently. Some people use profanity (yes even Christians), some get physical, some yell and scream, some throw things, some punch holes in walls, some hold it in until they erupt one day like a volcano and woe unto you if you happen to be within the blast radius.

These days there seem to be a host of things that can trigger ones anger especially if you have a short fuse. One of the situations in which many people fall short is when it involves driving. Two things that get my goat are traffic jams and bad drivers. The traffic jams are out of my control but I've been guilty myself of bad driving on occasion. Society has even coined a phrase to go along with it, we call it "road rage" when people lose control of their temper while driving. There has been a lot of property damage, personal injury, and even deaths as a result of traffic related anger.

   The truth is some days it doesn't take much to set us off! It could be as simple as a long line at the bank or grocery store. (Or, watching your favorite football team lose a game.) How about being on the losing end of a game you participated in? While they're all very minor things, they can create major havoc in the life of a person who's not in control of their emotions. Anger will cause you to manifest behavior that is not consistent with your character. There are still some incidents from my past that I'm embarrassed about which happened as a result of me losing my temper.

   With all that being said we need to find the solutions in God's word that will assist us in learning to manage our anger. James

1:19-20 says, "So then, my beloved
brethren, let every man be swift to hear,
slow to speak, slow to wrath; for the wrath
of man does not produce the righteousness
of God." If our anger or wrath doesn't
produce God's righteousness we should
probably all pay more attention to what it
does produce.

   In I Samuel chapter 25, with the exception
of verse 1 which speaks about the death of
the prophet Samuel, a story is told about
David and his temper. The three main
characters in the chapter are David whose
name means Beloved, Nabal whose name
means fool, and his wife Abigail whose
name means strength or joy of my father.
As the incident unfolds we find Nabal and
his servants shearing sheep in the
wilderness. The bible tells us that he was a
very rich man and that he was of the family
of Caleb. He apparently inherited his wealth
from the household of Caleb because Maon
where he lived, and Carmel where he did

business, were close to Hebron, the land conquered by Caleb many years prior. Seeing how the name Nabal means 'fool' it just goes to show that you can have a fool even in a good family.

During the sheep shearing festivities David sends ten of his men to Nabal to request a gift as a reward for the protection he had given his men while they were camped together in the wilderness. Perhaps Nabal was not a God fearing man since the bible says in Psalms 14:1, (The fool has said in his heart, "There is no God.") I say that because of his ungodly response to David's men. Not only were they refused but they were treated spitefully and Nabal pretended to not even know who David was. When the men reported to David how disrespectfully they were treated he was furious. His anger boiled over as he prepared 400 men to go and slaughter Nabal and every male, young and old in his family. Only the grace and wisdom of Nabal's wife Abigail spared him from being killed, and spared David from committing mass murder that day. David was prepared that day as Abigail put it,' to come to bloodshed by avenging himself!' But the bible says in Romans 12:19, Beloved, do not avenge yourselves, but rather give place to wrath; for it is written, "Vengeance is Mine, I will repay," says the Lord. Even King David, (The man after God's own heart) was capable of losing his temper.

There are many lessons that can be learned from this chapter. I'd like to examine just a few of them. First of all, there is the lesson of *trying to control outcome*. Let me begin by saying as a man of faith I believe that in certain situations under the right conditions one can reasonably expect God to move and produce favorable outcomes. We first need to begin from a position of faith. We also need to be aligned with God's plan and God's will. With these things in place it makes sense to trust Him for a particular result. I wouldn't necessarily say we can control the outcome but we can certainly have a strong influence on it.

   When I consider the details of this chapter there are things that jump out at me, one of them being David's attempt to control outcome. We all know David to be a man who was in tune with the Spirit of God but I'm not sure he was in this particular situation. It seems unlikely to me that he wouldn't have known what kind of man Nabal was. In I Samuel 25:25 Abigail says to David, "Please, let not my lord regard this scoundrel Nabal. For as is his name (fool), so is he." That suggests to me that David was aware of the meaning of his name and likely his character as well. So why would he enter into an unspoken and unwritten agreement expecting a little "quid pro quo" from a fool? There was probably the pressure of trying to provide for the hundreds of followers he had. Notice that he sent the ten men on the day of sheep shearing hoping Nabal would be in good enough spirits to repay them for the kindness they had shown his men. But truthfully, it's bad business to expect a fool to do the right thing.

It just doesn't add up that David would expect favorable outcome when dealing with a fool. Proverbs 18:6 says, "A fool's lips enter into contention, and his mouth calls for blows." We shouldn't be surprised when an ungodly person says things that get under our skin. It's as though Abigail were saying to David in verse 25, "You know how he is so why are you surprised by his behavior?" My advice is to remember that God is responsible for the outcome no matter what we do. In I Corinthians 3:6 the Apostle Paul says, "I planted, Apollos watered, but God gave the increase." That tells me that even in ministry related duties it's God who controls the outcome not you or me. We set ourselves up for anger and frustration when we try to control outcome. None of us are exempt from this lesson because we all from time to time try to control outcome and lose our temper when the desired result is not achieved.

The second thing is the lesson of *feeling disrespected*. This can be a very dangerous place to be because the root of these feelings is our pride. The word of God says in James 4:6, "God resists the proud, but gives grace to the humble." We only resist things we have a desire for. Anything I don't desire requires no resisting on my part. So the word is saying that God wants to do something on our behalf but pride will cause Him to resist the desire to help us. David's anger was fueled by the mentality that says, "Who does this fool (Nabal) think I am?" or "He must not know who he's dealing with!" or "Nobody talks to me like that!" Sound familiar? It should because we've all been there.

Our pride will make us believe we're more important than we really are. It will tell us we should be excluded from enduring such things. It's what says, "I won't allow this to happen to me!" But the reality is that God has allowed it to happen to us so who are we to say whether it should or shouldn't have happened? What really chapped David's hide more than anything was that this man had the audacity to disrespect him in front of his men. How many times have we lost our cool when we felt that someone had disrespected us? Maybe it was one of your children, or a co-worker or supervisor. Perhaps it was your spouse. Usually our response is "I'm not having it!" and we proceed to overreact. Think about it, David wasn't simply contemplating fighting he was prepared to commit murder of not just one man but every male in Nabal's family. His goal was to destroy his posterity and remove his name from the face of the earth. The punishment didn't fit the crime!

Let's face it being disrespected hurts. It hurts a lot! But I would venture to say if that's the worst thing that ever happens to you in life, you're going to have a pretty awesome life. Our goal in these situations is to not make a mountain out of a molehill as they say. Don't allow yourself to go on a mission to repay evil for evil. Jesus said in Matthew 5:44, "But I say to you, love your enemies, bless those who curse you, do good to those who hate you, and pray for those who spitefully use you and persecute you," I Peter 5:5 says we are to be "clothed with humility" That speaks to me because I never leave my house unless I'm clothed. So if I'm clothed with humility that suggests its part of my daily routine. If I'm walking in that clothing I'll be better prepared for handling those feelings of disrespect.

The third and last thing is the lesson of *being open to hear God's voice*. Although I have elaborated on David's failure in that circumstance I can't help but be impressed with his ability to remain open to hearing God's voice. That is not an easy task when you're boiling mad. The fact that he listened to Abigail at that moment speaks to the depth of his relationship with God. When it's all said and done it will be the substance of our relationship with the Lord that dictates how we come out of angry situations.

You and I must always strive for the ability to quiet ourselves long enough to hear the voice of the Holy Spirit in the midst of our anger. Because the word of God says that He speaks with "a still small voice." (I Kings 19:12) That's what makes David's attitude so amazing! In the midst of all that fury he somehow found a way to listen to the voice of God in that moment. I wish I could say that's how I've always handled myself but that would be far from true. If we're going to be that kind of person it's going to take a life of consistency in the word of God, in prayer and fasting, and the fellowship of the saints, and that's just the beginning!

When we're overcome with rage God will send an Abilgail our way. An Abigail can pour cool water on a hot head. An Abigail can remain neutral while seeking a peaceful resolution for all parties involved. Thanks to her faithfulness to God's plan David was convinced that he should trust God for the outcome. She gave David what he really wanted, a means by which he could take care of his followers. She brought food and the necessary items needed to alleviate his stress and calm his spirit. We would all do well to learn how to listen for God's voice in the midst of frustration and not take matters into our own hands.

When David trusted God for the outcome, let go of the feelings of being disrespected, and listened to the voice of God, Nabal suffered a stroke that day and died ten days later. He then proposed to Abigail and took her to be his wife. The truth is if we just let God handle things they always work out for our good (Romans 8:28). The sin David was about to commit would have cast an ugly shadow on his life. Not only because of what he did personally, but that he was prepared to drag his men into the sin also. So the next time you're in a similar situation, wait for your Abigail. Oh and by the way, your Abigail might be a man.

Three Things to Remember

1. Don't have an overly optimistic expectation about how people respond to an act of kindness. You'll open the door to anger when you don't get the result you expected.
2. Don't take matters into your own hands when it comes to getting justice. God says, "vengeance is mine, I will repay" Romans 12:19
3. Always remain open to hear God's voice even when you're angry. Hearing God's voice is the first step. Obeying God's voice is what really matters.

Chapter Two
"A Lesson on Past Mistakes"

There comes a point in time when every one of us reflects on our past and we find mistakes we wish we hadn't made. We replay the scene over and over in our minds while thinking if only I had handled it a different way. I've always shared with people in counseling that you can't go back and fix yesterday. But you can fix today so your tomorrows won't be like your yesterdays. (If only I could remember that advice when it comes to my own life) In all honesty, more often than not I do apply that truth to my life. Since we began this book studying the great King David, let's continue with his example for just a while longer.

I want to draw your attention to the narrative involving David and the Holy Bread found in I Samuel chapters 21 and 22. The relevant characters for the purpose of examining this story are David, Ahimelech the priest whose name means brother of the king, King Saul whose name means asked for; demanded or required, Abiathar the son of Ahimelech whose name means plenty or father of plenty, and Doeg the Edomite whose name means fearful, anxious or sorrowful.

The bible tells us that David went to the city of Nob while on the run to escape from King Saul. Nob was a city given to the priests and their families in accordance with Mosaic Law. There was apparently a place for worship and sacrificing and Ahimelech was the overseer. When David arrives Ahimelech immediately notices something strange when he sees David alone and not traveling with an entourage considering that he was at that time the king's son-in-law. When he questions David about it the lying begins. David's response is that he was on a secret mission for the king that required such urgency it left him alone and without food. It's sad that even as Christians we can so easily be given to dishonesty. Sometimes all it takes is for someone to ask a question we're not prepared to answer and the lies just start to flow from our mouths.

David then begins asking for bread and he is told by the priest that the only bread available is the showbread that is presented to the Lord. After David tells Ahimelech that he and his men had been kept from women for the past three days, the priest agrees to give him the Holy Bread. (Apparently since the bread was consecrated, those who ate it needed to be consecrated as well) At this point in the story we are introduced to an Edomite man named Doeg, the chief of the herdsmen who belonged to Saul. (The Edomites are of the descendants of Esau) We're told that he was there that day "detained before the Lord" We could speculate for quite some time on what exactly he was doing there but suffice it to say he was there against his will. We can draw that conclusion based on the word "detained" For me no matter how I look at that word, it doesn't convey anything positive. The dictionary defines it as "keeping someone from proceeding; hold back" or "keep someone in official custody, typically for questioning about a crime or in politically sensitive matters" So that begs the question, how or why would someone be detained before the Lord? We'll talk more about that later but I say that anyone in the house of God feeling detained is someone you should probably keep an eye on.

What's worth mentioning is that in chapter 22 we find out that he saw David and David saw him. A fact that is critical to what unfolds in this account. David's attention is then turned to his need for a weapon and he asks Ahimelech if there is a sword on hand? I can only imagine how ridiculous David sounded telling the priest that he left in such a hurry he forgot to bring his sword. At any rate Ahimelech offers him the sword of Goliath. (One that certainly David had a history with seeing how he used it to cut off Goliath's head) He happily receives the sword and leaves the city of Nob and goes to the Philistine city of Gath and into the presence of king Achish. When the Philistines recognize him he then pretends to be insane and they evict him from their city.

I want to deviate from the main subject matter just briefly to make a point. David, like so many people who come to church, came to Ahimelech under false pretenses. As a man of God when people don't tell you the truth you can only minister to them based on the information you've been given. But no matter what they tell you, as a minister you can only give them the two things they need the most. The Bread (Jesus is the bread of life) and the Sword (The word of God) with those two things they can become more than conquerors. As Pastor's we give people the Bread and the Sword regularly but many of them walk out of the church house and as soon as trouble comes they act crazy. So remember man of God no matter what kind of stories the members of your congregation tell you, give them the Bread and the Sword. If they recognize the value of what you've given them they can be successful in whatever they do!

In I Samuel verses 6-23 we see the outcome of David's actions that day. We find King Saul lamenting the fact that he's unaware of David's whereabouts and none of his men seem to be concerned with helping him find David. We then discover that Doeg has been released from his detention and volunteers information about not only David but Ahimelech as well. Doeg twists the story (lies) and tells Saul that Ahimelech has partnered with David and supplied him with food and weapons to help his cause. The end result is that Saul goes to the city of Nob, accuses Ahimelech of treason and sentences him and the entire city to death. Since none of Saul's men felt comfortable executing the priests, Doeg volunteered to carry out the killings and he proceeded to kill eighty-five priests and their families.

Only one man escaped Doeg's sword that day and it was Ahimelech's son Abiathar. He fled the scene and caught up with David and told him what had happened. Here's what David's response was in I Samuel 22:22-23, So David said to Abiathar, "I knew that day, when Doeg the Edomite was there, that he would surely tell Saul. I have caused the death of all the persons of your father's house. Stay with me; do not fear. For he who seeks my life seeks your life, but with me you shall be safe." Is it just me or does it sound like David basically said, "I knew something like this might happen when I saw Doeg that day, but I had to do what I had to do! Sorry about that, my bad!" David just made a mistake that cost the lives of an entire city and he tells Abiathar he knew when he saw Doeg that he would surely tell Saul. What I'm trying to understand is how come Abiathar doesn't punch David right in his mouth? How does someone tell you they're responsible for the death of your entire family and you're okay with it? Abiathar may be one of the most faithful and humble men in the bible. I say that because in I Samuel 23:6 it says, "Now it happened, when Abiathar the son of Ahimelech fled to David at Keilah, that he went down with an ephod in his hand." The ephod was one of the articles used by the priests to call on God. Here's the picture, Doeg is slaughtering everyone in the city. There's death and the screaming voices of his loved ones all around and somehow he's thinking "I can't leave without the ephod!" Abiathar was still focused on his calling. He knew with his father and all the others dead he was the only one left who could carry on the ministry as priest before the Lord. He actually stayed with David and functioned in his priestly capacity even after David had become king.

(Running Red Lights)

I want to discuss the traffic signal and how it relates to the narrative of David and the Holy Bread. In the early 1900's there was an African American inventor named Garrett A. Morgan. He was the son of slaves who possessed a sixth grade education and yet found a way to impact the world. He was responsible for several inventions including the gas mask. What I'd like to focus on is his contribution to the modern day traffic signal.

History says that Garrett Morgan witnessed a traffic accident in 1922 that inspired him to modify the design of the traffic signal that existed at the time. With traffic laws, driver's license and DMV's in the early stages of development as automobiles were being introduced into society, accidents were all too common. Without an adequate means to govern traffic there was property damage, personal injury and death in many instances. The motivation for his invention was saving lives.

Our modern day traffic signal communicates three primary messages, they are; green for go, red for stop, and contrary to popular belief yellow means prepare to stop. I know most folks seem to think yellow means "step on it!" but that is not true. When drivers fail to adhere to those signals often times it leads to property damage and injury or fatality as a result. In many cases the person who runs the red light comes out unscathed while the vehicles behind them suffer the consequences of their decision.

When David said in I Samuel 22:22, "I knew that day, when Doeg the Edomite was there, that he would surely tell Saul." That was the yellow light that quickly turned red! There will be times in our life when the plans we have will sometimes intersect with a red light from God. David's decision to run a red light that day cost the lives of an entire city. How many times in your life has God asked you to stop doing something and you refused only to discover your decision hurt others. When I allowed drugs and alcohol to control my life the Lord was constantly putting red lights in front of me and I continued to run through them and hurt a lot of people in the process.

David's selfish desire to accomplish his own agenda caused him to not only use dishonesty but to also disregard potential harm to others. It's true that David could not have known how badly Doeg would misrepresent him to Saul but he knew Doeg would tell. David and Doeg shared something in common that day they were both being dishonest in an attempt to get what they wanted. David wanted food and weapons. Doeg wanted to earn some favor with the king. As an Edomite Doeg belonged to a people who were at that time subservient to Israel but still maintained favorable treatment because of Mosaic Law. Deuteronomy 23:7 says, "You shall not abhor an Edomite, for he is your brother." I know that David had no intention of hurting anyone else like practically everyone who runs a red light. But if you happened to receive a citation for running a red light, the citation will be based on your action not your intention. And even if you get away without the citation but cause other vehicles to crash, does that make you any less responsible?

The bottom line is to remember that red lights are not permanent! It is a temporary stop. Every red light is followed by a green light. When your plans intersect with a red light from God know that it doesn't mean quit, it means wait! We would all do well to refrain from running red lights. When we do that we put into practice Philippians 2:4, "Let each of you look out not only for his own interests, but also for the interests of others."

Three Things to Remember

1. Never use dishonesty to achieve your goals. The end doesn't justify the means.
2. Recognize the spiritual traffic signals in your life. In many cases the person who runs the red light causes more damage to others than he himself suffers.
3. Remember that a red light is a temporary stop not a permanent one. Every red light is always followed by a green light. Wait until God gives you the "All Clear" sign.

Chapter Three
"A Lesson on Low Self-Esteem"

I thank God for bringing me into a ministry like Victory Outreach International because of the opportunities I've had to work with so many people at the grass roots level. One of our core ministries is our Christian Recovery Homes and I've had the privilege of directing two, one in the San Fernando Valley, and one in Washington, DC. Men and women typically come into the Recovery Home broken and defeated by their battle with addiction. (A battle in which they were on the losing end for a number of years) One of the by-products that can be a residual effect of that lifestyle is low self-esteem.

Like many others when I entered the Recovery Home in 1987 I had lost the confidence I once possessed to believe I could succeed in life. My self-esteem was damaged by the many setbacks I'd suffered as a result of my addiction to crack cocaine. That, along with a host of other issues had combined to make it all the more difficult for me to accept the fact that God wanted to use my life. It was only through a steady diet of prayer and God's word that I was able to overcome my spiritual disability.

In II Samuel 4:4 the bible speaks about a young man named Mephibosheth whose name means to scatter; to exterminate; or shame, the son of Jonathan, the son of King Saul. The scripture says, "Jonathan, Saul's son, had a son who was lame in his feet. He was five years old when the news about Saul and Jonathan came from Jezreel; and his nurse took him up and fled. And it happened, as she made haste to flee, that he fell and became lame. His name was Mephibosheth." Talk about a tough day! As if it weren't bad enough that he lost his father and grandfather, he's also left incapacitated as a result of his nurses mishap. He goes from being the son of a prince to becoming a cripple who now must depend on others to take care of him. I would imagine that Mephibosheth felt as if God had abandoned him and left him to suffer for the rest of his life. How hard would it be for any of us to find a silver lining with a cloud like that hanging above our heads?

Fortunately God's word says "I will never leave you nor forsake you." (Hebrews 13:5) He has a plan and a purpose for every human being that He tirelessly pursues through the work of the Holy Spirit. The Lord will not renege on His promise regardless of what path we find ourselves on. It doesn't matter if we're on that path by choice or by chance. His desire to bless us, or use us, isn't based on our goodness, but on His! David said in Psalm 40:2, "He also brought me up out of a horrible pit, out of the miry clay, and set my feet upon a rock, and established my steps." The good news is that He'll do the same for you and me!

In II Samuel chapter nine we find King David searching for an heir of Jonathan so that he might show him the kindness of God. He says in verse one, "Is there anyone who is left of the house of Saul, that I may show him kindness for Jonathan's sake?" He finds Mephibosheth living with a man named Ziba (plant; appointed) who had fifteen sons and twenty servants. After years of feeling like a burden to those he depended on, his disability has him believing he's useless and without hope. His response to King David's desire to bless him was, "What is your servant, that you should look upon such a dead dog as I?" (Verse 8) Not only did he feel God wouldn't bless him, he didn't feel he deserved God's blessing. That's low self-esteem! Clearly whatever zeal for life or hope he may have had for a future had been given up on long ago.

Many people find themselves traveling that road. That road you're on when you begin to believe life has dealt you a bad hand and there's nothing you can do about it. Without the right kind of help and support a person can adapt a mentality that says, "I will be miserable and hopeless for the rest of my life. I guess this is how my life is supposed to be. There's no reason to believe I can ever be happy." I don't think Mephibosheth believed his life could ever change for the good, but God's love never gave up on him. He lost everything in one day, and now in one day he was about to have everything restored! He was understandably doubtful about his fortunes changing but when David showed up that day he was about the hit the Holy Ghost lotto! If you give God a chance He'll pour out His love on you with such great measure that you can't help but feel valued and loved!

What Mephibosheth experienced that day was the joy of being adopted into the family of God! King David made a declaration that day stating Mephibosheth would eat continually at his table along with him and his sons. And if that wasn't good enough he appointed Ziba, his fifteen sons and his twenty servants, to serve Mephibosheth! I'm pretty sure that the lame man's outlook on life was dramatically changed that day. When God shows us His, *storge love* (pronounced stor-gay, which is Greek for belonging) our self-esteem is monumentally improved! Mephibosheth went from feeling left out or shamed, to knowing he had been brought in! The lesson we can take from this story is that God will never give up on us even when we've given up on ourselves. Also God's word is true when He says, "And the Lord will make you the head and not the tail." (Deuteronomy 28:13) Mephibosheth woke up that morning as the tail, and went to bed that night as the head! His life was injected with self-esteem!

In Luke 19:1-10, the story is told of a man named Zacchaeus whose name means pure or justified. The bible describes him as a wealthy tax collector. That description makes sense because it is commonly believed that most tax collectors in those days would overcharge the people in order line their own pockets. What is worth taking note of is that in addition to his financial status the bible includes his physical stature. We are told that he's short. If you read the entire bible (I have several times) you will find very few instances in which a person's physical characteristics are mentioned. I find it interesting that the Holy Spirit moved Luke to include this detail in his story.

There are only two characters named in this narrative, Jesus, and Zacchaeus. We are told that Jesus is passing through the city of Jericho and not surprisingly He's drawing a crowd. It was a common occurrence in those days for large groups of people to gather whenever Jesus showed up. In speaking about Zacchaeus verse 4 says, "So he ran ahead and climbed up into a sycamore tree to see Him, for He was going to pass that way." Too short to see over the crowd he has to elevate himself just so he could catch a glimpse of Jesus passing by. When I want to connect with Jesus I have to do a little elevating myself. First I elevate my prayer then my prayer elevates me! Once I've prayed I stand taller and gain clarity to see over the obstacles and see Jesus! The fact that he ran also gives us a peak into the personality of this man. It speaks of his desperation to achieve his goal. But his running and climbing paid off as we see in verses 5-6 it says, "And when Jesus came to the place, He looked up and saw him and said to him, 'Zacchaeus, make haste and come down, for today I must stay at your house.' So he made haste and came down, and received Him joyfully."

It is in those two verses where a miracle takes place! What impresses me the most isn't so much what does happen, but what doesn't happen. There's no mention of Jesus inquiring from anyone as to what the man's name was. As it turns out Zacchaeus thought it was he who was pursuing Jesus, when in fact it was Jesus who was pursuing Zacchaeus! And just like in this instance, He knows your name! We all from time to time speak of finding Jesus when in fact we're the ones who were lost!

Another interesting fact is that Luke tells us that it was a sycamore tree Zacchaeus climbed. I asked myself, why did God inspire him to include that seemingly insignificant detail? Do I really need to know what kind of tree it was? Couldn't he have just said he climbed a tree? Those are the questions that led me to exegete the word "sycamore" to find out if there was any deeper meaning. What I discovered is there were three Greek words used to translate the word sycamore. The first word is *sukomoria – soo-kom-o-rah-yah* which means "the sycamore" or fig tree, the second word is the root word *sukon – soo-kon* which means a fig tree, and third is the word *suke – soo-kay* which means a fig tree. It seems to me that a more accurate description would've been fig tree. Based on that information what I see is a man hiding behind fig leaves. (Sound familiar?) Adam and Eve used fig leaves in an attempt to hide their sin or prevent being exposed before God. Once sin entered their lives they didn't feel comfortable in God's presence like they did before. Their self-esteem had been damaged. As a sinner Zacchaeus didn't feel deserving to receive the love of God. I believe his being short also referred to his feeling small and insignificant. Not even fig leaves can prevent God from seeing the sin in our lives. It's also true that the sin in our lives won't prevent God from extending His great love to us because He has the power to cleanse us from sin!

I would imagine that of all the people in Jericho that day Zacchaeus would've been the last choice to receive a home visit from Jesus. Tax collectors were not the most popular people in those days. (They're not very popular today either.) The bible says in verse 6, "they all complained saying, 'He has gone to be a guest with a man who is a sinner.'" We're not told who "they" are but suffice it to say "they" were the haters. Apparently haters have been around for a long time. With Jesus in his house he probably felt like the biggest man in town. It likely was a huge boost to his self-esteem. He made a public declaration of his repentance and vowed to repay fourfold the people he had cheated. So, even if you feel small, and undeserving, and are embarrassed about the sin in your life like Zacchaeus. If you're desperate enough and pure in your motives you can run and climb your way to Jesus, and He will reward you

with life everlasting! Jesus also made a
public declaration that day in verses 9-10,
And Jesus said to him, "Today salvation has
come to this house, because he also is a son
of Abraham; for the Son of Man has come
to seek and to save that which was lost."
"Amazing grace how sweet the sound that
saved a wretch like me, I once was lost but
now I'm found, was blind but now I see."

Three Things to Remember

1. Material goods won't cure the ailment of the soul. Small doesn't equal insignificant. Popularity with people or the lack thereof doesn't earn one favor with God.
2. A demonstration of desperation will always get God's attention. His climbing demonstrated his willingness to get over his problems. His running demonstrated his willingness to put things behind him.
3. Having sin in our lives doesn't disqualify us from being called as long as were willing to repent. Repentance opens the door for a change in perspective. It is the lost person that Jesus seeks.

Chapter Four
"A Lesson on Overcoming Discouragement"

I want to talk about one of the most misunderstood and misrepresented men in the New Testament. That man is John Mark. His two names combined have individual meanings, John means Jehovah has been gracious, and Mark means a large hammer or polite. Over the years I have heard preachers have a field day on this man focusing exclusively on his failure while ignoring his strength. He is unfortunately known mostly for leaving the mission filed while traveling with Paul and Barnabas. There are no specifics given as to why he left but popular opinion is that John Mark didn't have the backbone needed to finish the assignment. Truthfully, that line of thinking may have some merit.

John Mark first appears in Acts 12:12, "So, when he had considered this, he came to the house of Mary, the mother of John whose surname was Mark, where many were gathered together praying." This is where he and others were praying for the Apostle Peter while he was in jail. (I don't believe it's too much of a stretch to assume he was in attendance since it was his mother's house) After Peter's miraculous deliverance from the jail cell he immediately goes to the house where the prayer meeting is taking place. This tells me that he had a connection with not only Paul but Peter as well. In fact he was probably connected with Peter prior to traveling with Paul and Barnabas. I Peter 5:13 says, "She who is in Babylon, elect together with you, greets you; and so does Mark my son." His reference to John Mark as his son sheds some light on their relationship. It gives the impression that John Mark was one of Peter's disciples. It also tells me that he was a praying man. If you're going to overcome discouragement you'll need to be a person of prayer.

The next time he's mentioned is in Acts 12:25 when he becomes a traveling companion with Paul and Barnabas, "And Barnabas and Saul returned from Jerusalem when they had fulfilled their ministry, and they also took with them John whose surname was Mark." One of the other details about him is that he was the cousin of Barnabas. I would imagine that his being related to Barnabas played a role in his being invited along on the missionary trip. After all, Barnabas, whose name means "son of encouragement" would've certainly wanted to be an encouragement to his cousin as he was to the church and to the Apostle Paul.

He next appears on the pages of scripture in Acts 13, verses 2-5 say, (As they ministered to the Lord and fasted, the Holy Spirit said, "Now separate to Me Barnabas and Saul for the work to which I have called them." Then, having fasted and prayed, and laid hands on them, they sent them away. So, being sent out by the Holy Spirit, they went down to Seleucia, and from there they sailed to Cyprus. And when they arrived in Salamis, they preached the word of God in the synagogues of the Jews. They also had John as their assistant.)

It was in Cyprus that Paul and Barnabas were given the opportunity to minister to the proconsul Sergius Paulus. (A proconsul functioned as the governor over a Roman province) In Acts 13:7 we're told that he called for Barnabas and Paul so he could hear the word of God. We're also told in verse 8 that a sorcerer name Elymas withstood them and attempted to hinder the proconsul from receiving Christ. Verses 9-12 tell us that Paul rebuked the sorcerer and spoke a curse over him in which he was subjected to a temporary blindness. As a result of that miracle the proconsul believed and came to Christ.

It is however in the very next verse, Acts 13:13, that John Mark earned his reputation as a quitter. "Now when Paul and his party set sail from Paphos, they came to Perga in Pamphylia; and John, departing from them, returned to Jerusalem." It is here where we are left to speculate on John Mark's reasons for leaving the mission field. It's an unfortunate situation to be in when people are left to speculate about your motives for what you and I do or don't do. It has been my experience that people generally in those times don't give the benefit of the doubt. I'm not sure what the psychology is behind it but more often than not people think the worst when they're left to fill in the blanks.

One thing that can be said with certainty is the Apostle Paul didn't accept John Mark's reason for leaving as valid and the evidence for that claim is found in Acts 15:36-41. "Then after some days Paul said to Barnabas, 'Let us now go back and visit our brethren in every city where we have preached the word of the Lord, and see how they are doing.' Now Barnabas was determined to take with them John called Mark. But Paul insisted that they should not take with them the one who had departed from them in Pamphylia, and had not gone with them to the work. Then the contention became so sharp that they parted from one another. And so Barnabas took Mark and sailed to Cyprus; but Paul chose Silas and departed, being commended by the brethren to the grace of God. And he went through Syria and Cilicia, strengthening the churches."

Here is where I'd like to share my observation on what took place that day. We see Paul and Barnabas who had been friends and co-laborers in the ministry for quite some time. In fact it was Barnabas who was an encouragement to Paul when he first got saved by speaking up for him to the disciples who didn't trust Paul. They get into a heated discussion (argument) because Barnabas has a desire to give his cousin a second chance. Basically, Paul's position was "He'll get no second chance from me! Any team that includes John Mark is a team I want no part of! I don't believe in him! I think he's of no value! If you want him so bad you take him and both of you can go your own way without me!" If I'm John Mark and I'm hearing this, I think I'd be feeling very discouraged. Regardless of why he left the previous mission, does it seem fair that he should be treated this harshly? Since we serve the God of another chance, shouldn't we be a people always willing to give others another chance? If God took that same approach with us how many of us would be where we are today? My answers to those three questions are, no to the first, yes to the second, and not many to the third.

When I visualize the events that took place that day I see a young man who would've undoubtedly been very discouraged by Paul's attitude. It reminds me of when I was just a boy and we'd go to the schoolyard or the park to play sports. . Usually there was one kid who wasn't very good at sports but nevertheless loved to participate. It often resulted in their being the kid no one wanted on their team. To make matters worse the team captains would argue in front of them about why they don't' want them on their team. Even to the point of choosing a total stranger to avoid them. I would sometimes feel so bad for the kid who's being left out but my desire to compete and win was so strong that I went along with the crowd and excluded them also. Talk about feeling discouraged. No one likes feeling unwanted and unappreciated.

I realize the above analogy doesn't equate to the seriousness of John Mark's situation but being rejected hurts no matter how it happens. ("The same areas of our brain become activated when we experience rejection as when we experience physical pain. That's why even small rejections hurt more than we think they should, because they elicit literal (albeit, emotional) pain." Psychologist Guy Winch) Being rejected not only hurts but can trigger feelings of discouragement. The Apostle Paul says in Ephesians 4:29 "Let no corrupt word proceed out of your mouth, but what is good for necessary edification, that it may impart grace to the hearers." I don't believe Paul said anything edifying to John Mark that day. It just goes to show even leaders can make mistakes in judgment.

The beautiful thing about John Mark is he didn't quit on his relationship with God. He believed, as did Barnabas, he was more prepared for the mission field the second time and it seems he was right. The way I see it his resilience helped keep him in line with God's will. Perhaps it was meant to work out that way because now instead of one missionary team there were two. Thanks to the split between Paul and Barnabas they could now cover twice as much ground.

The bible says that Barnabas and Mark sailed to Cyprus. It was at Cyprus where the incident between Paul and the sorcerer took place. I submit that it's possible something happened in Cyprus that caused John Mark to leave when they reached Pamphylia. Could it be that he was returning to the scene of the crime so to speak? Is there a possibility that God allowed him to return to Cyprus and conquer whatever caused him trouble the first time around? I believe it's possible. I have no evidence to support my opinion other than the clues I draw from the scripture so I guess it's open to interpretation. But if we follow that line of thinking we can assume he was allowed to prove himself and put that discouragement under his feet.

What I can say with certainty is that the Apostle Paul changed his mind about John Mark eventually and saw value in him. In II Timothy 4:11 he says, "Only Luke is with me. Get Mark and bring him with you, for he is useful to me for ministry." It also shows that John Mark was a man of great character. He was capable of overlooking what happened between him and the Apostle Paul and still be a help to him in his final days. And just in case you're still not convinced that he was a great man of God, the gospel of Mark was ultimately written by, that's right John Mark! So if you get discouraged along the way by people who don't believe in you take heart, you're in good company. Even if the one who doesn't believe in you is a leader, just do what the Lord commands you and He will change their heart in His time!

In the end I guess Jehovah was gracious to John Mark and he politely hammered that point home by his actions.

Three Things to Remember

1. Failure doesn't have to be final. We must always be prepared to bounce back with or without the support of friends.
2. Don't allow a setback to dissuade you from fulfilling God's purpose for your life. Even if people of influence stop believing in you, believe in yourself (in Christ).
3. Your words won't convince your critics, your actions will. Stay humble and forgive those who doubted you knowing that it was your actions that fueled their doubts.

Chapter Five
"A Lesson on Losing Faith"

I want to take another look at David, the great king of Israel who God describes as "a man after My own heart," (Acts 13:22) For the most part David is a shining example in the scriptures of leadership, humility, love, and faith. But even the greatest of men have their struggles and are desperately in need of God's grace. It seems that after trusting God for deliverance from King Saul over and over again, David began to have doubts about the Lord's power to protect him from the snare of death.

In I Samuel 27:1 it reads, And David said in his heart, "Now I shall perish someday by the hand of Saul. There is nothing better for me than that I should speedily escape to the land of the Philistines; and Saul will despair of me, to seek me anymore in any part of Israel. So I shall escape out of his hand."

This statement seems so out of character for David because if there was one thing he was good at, it was trusting God.

I guess it's safe to say he grew tired of being pursued by King Saul and as Vince Lombardi the Hall of Fame coach of the Green Bay Packers once said, "Fatigue makes cowards of us all." It may explain why David would choose to align himself with the Philistines of all people. I'll go out on a limb and say that most of us have either witnessed or experienced an unhealthy partnership during a season of failing faith. From I Samuel 27:1 through 28:2 we're given insight into the allegiance David formed with Achish whose name means serpent charmer or a hard place, the king of Gath. It wasn't he alone who went into the land of the Philistines for safety but he also brought along his six hundred men with their wives and children. (For some reason, not given in the scriptures, his trip to Gath turns out completely opposite of his visit in I Samuel 21:10-14 where he was immediately recognized, and had to pretend madness to get out of town.)

Instead he is received joyfully by King Achish and given the city of Ziklag as a residence for him, his wives, and the families of his men. Ziklag means winding, a measure of oppression, or enveloped in grief. It's here where things get interesting and the picture of his lost faith gets clearer. It was bad enough that he chose to abandon his faith, but the decision is made worse by the fact that he brought others with him. It was no different for David than it would be for anyone who decided to walk away from the Lord. If you go back to world you must try to fit in with the environment you've entered. While David was in Ziklag he couldn't profess loyalty to the God of Israel or else he'd be rejected by the Philistines.

In chapter 27:7 it says, "Now the time that David dwelt in the country of the Philistines was one full year and four months." So for almost a year and a half there was no worshiping God, no praying to God, because in order to live among the Philistines, he had to pretend to be a Philistine. Most historians don't attribute any of David's Psalms or prayers to this period of his life.

To further make this point let's look at chapter 27 verses 8-12, And David and his men went up and raided the Geshurites, the Girzites, and the Amalekites. For those nations were the inhabitants of the land from of old, as you got to Shur, even as far as the land of Egypt. Whenever David attacked the land, he left neither man nor woman alive, but took away the sheep, the oxen, the donkeys, the camels, and the apparel, and returned and came to Achish. Then Achish would say, "Where have you made raid today?" And David would say, "Against the southern area of Judah, or against the southern area of the Jerahmeelites, or against the southern area of the Kenites." David would save neither man nor woman alive, to bring news to Gath, saying, "Lest they should inform on us, saying, 'Thus David did.'" And thus was his behavior all the time he dwelt in the country of the Philistines. So Achish believed David, saying, "He has made his people Israel utterly abhor him; therefore he will be my servant forever."

Basically, what these verses are saying is that David led his men on raids of some of Israel's known enemies, left no one alive, all the while pretending he was attacking Israel. The scripture says he left no one alive so they couldn't tell king Achish what he was really doing. I realize that often times God would instruct his people to destroy completely their enemies when going out to conquer. The problem I see is there doesn't seem to be anything that suggests he was acting under a direct command from God, it looks like he's doing his own thing.

That's the problem with drifting away from God and giving the enemy space in our hearts. The devil will always ask you to go further than you want to go, and do things you never thought you'd have to do. For David that lesson was driven home in a way that he'd never forget! Whenever people walk away from God and dance with the devil, he will ultimately attempt to take you somewhere you just can't go! If you're a person who has known God intimately and walked with him faithfully for a length of time, the conviction of the Holy Spirit will still prick your heart. God will never give up on us! Hallelujah!

In the 29th chapter of I Samuel God brought David to the "Valley of Decision." The Philistines were on their way to fight against King Saul and his son Jonathan in the battle on Mount Gilboa. This was in fact the place where Saul and Jonathan would die. Certainly this was not a fight David wanted to take part in. There's no way he would give himself to helping the Philistines kill Saul and Jonathan but now that he's been a servant of King Achsih for the past sixteen months, how can he walk away without drawing the ire of the Philistines? The answer is, he can't!

I love the fact that God has the power to get us out of the messes we get ourselves into. God's grace and favor knows no boundaries! It is my opinion that David at this point is agonizing over how to avoid going into battle against Saul and Jonathan. After all, had he wanted to kill King Saul he could've done it long ago on two separate occasions, but he chose to leave the kings life in God's hands. Now as he and his men travel with the Philistines on their way to the battle there has to be some conflict going on in his soul about his situation.

What happens next can only be explained as divine intervention!

After almost a year and a half of service to the king of Gath and his administration God steps in to bring David back to where he belongs. It seems that even though David had endeared himself to king Achish, when it really came down to it, the lords of the Philistines didn't trust David. The timing for them to voice their distrust couldn't have been better. The Philistines lords complain to the king that if David and his men are allowed to go with them he could turn against them in the battle and help Israel. Previously there had been no complaints about David and his men. I believe God stirred them up to deliver David from an awkward situation in which he would sin against God. In chapter 29:3 they said, "What are these Hebrews doing here?" While Achish defended David the Philistine lords insisted that David and his men be sent away. In verses 4-5 they say, "Make this fellow return, that he may go back to the place which you have appointed him, and do not let him go down to battle, lest in the battle he become our adversary. For with what could he reconcile himself to his master, if not with the heads of these men? Is this not David, of whom they sang to one another in dances, saying: 'Saul has slain his thousands, and David his ten thousands'?"

I find it interesting that it took them sixteen months to associate David with the killing of Goliath. And so the king, against his own desire, yields to the pressure of the Philistine lords and tells David he must leave. In verse 8 we see David pleading with the king as though he desired to lift his hand against Israel and its king. I believe it to be an attempt to keep up the front and not appear happy he was being relieved of duty. Verse 8 says, So David said to Achish, "But what have I done? And to this day what have you found in your servant as long as I have been with you, that I may not go and fight against the enemies of my lord the king?" (Seriously?) I guess David was also a pretty good actor! At any rate it worked and he and his men were released from their obligation to fight for the Philistines against Saul and Jonathan. But David still hadn't learned his lesson so God had to apply more pressure to bring him back to right standing in order that he might fulfill his destiny as the next king of Israel.

When people spend too much time away from the Lord they become insensitive to the voice of God and are prone to not receive His message clearly. David and his men made their way back to Ziklag. While Ziklag was their place of residence, it was nevertheless a gift from the enemy. It's important that when God brings us back from drifting in our relationship with Him that we relinquish everything associated with what caused us to lose faith. Although I'm sure Ziklag was a nice place it wasn't where David belonged. He belonged in

Jerusalem! I love how anytime someone in the bible goes to Jerusalem they are said to be going "up" to Jerusalem. And anytime someone leaves Jerusalem they are said to be going "down" from Jerusalem. So it's safe to say David went "down" to Ziklag, when God wanted him to go "up" to Jerusalem.

In chapter 30:1-2 we see God's hand guiding David back to where he belonged spiritually. The bible says, "Now it happened, when David and his men came to Ziklag, on the third day, that the Amalekites had invaded the south and Ziklag, attacked Ziklag and burned it with fire, and had taken captive the women and those who were there, from small to great; they did not kill anyone, but carried them away and went their way." Some of the greatest revelations men receive are birthed during times of great pain. Often it's in those times we hear God speak! The Amalekites had taken all of their wives, children and their possessions! When the crying finally stopped, (The bible says they had no more power to weep) David's men spoke of stoning him. After all, it was David who had led them away from God and into the arms of the Philistines. They probably sensed they were under the judgment of God and it was all David's fault!

Seeing that David was their leader I suppose he did bear some responsibility for where they were. It's my opinion that God was dealing with David and they were along for the ride. Thankfully, in verses 6- 7 David does something that was long overdue, he finally turned his heart back to God. The bible says, "But David strengthened himself in the Lord his God." Then David said to Abiathar the priest, Ahimelech's son, "Please bring the ephod here to me." And Abiathar brought the ephod to David. It took a year and four months but David finally reached the decision to trust the

Lord again and not lean on his own understanding. (Prov. 3:5)

   It was in that moment that David returned to his first love and his friend Abiathar the priest was right there to help him. You remember Abiathar? We talked about him in the second chapter. (The priest who escaped the edge of Doeg's sword in the city of Nob. The amazingly loyal man who managed to retrieve the ephod.) Thank God he did because they used it that day to call on the Lord! God told him, "Pursue, for you shall surely overtake them and without fail recover all."

   I would imagine it brought joy to Abiathar's heart to see the soon to be King David returning to being the man he agreed to follow the day he lost his family. Whenever we succumb to doubt and fear we lose faith, and it impacts those within our sphere of influence. Abiathar, as well as the six hundred men who followed David must have all felt a sense of relief when they saw him return to the Lord. Now instead of stoning him they're prepared to follow him again! If you've lost your faith today your family and friends are likely to be deeply concerned about your well being. Turn your heart back to Jesus and it will not only light up your life but theirs as well!

Thank God for friends like Abiathar who stand with us through the good times and the bad times and are ready and waiting to pray with us when we do like the prodigal son, and come to ourselves. (Luke 15:17) There will always be those who labor faithfully in obscurity that God uses to encourage us during difficult times in our lives. His retrieval of the ephod (I Samuel 23:6) gives insight into how committed he was to his role as priest.

Finally, there are the words "recover all" that God speaks to David. I believe those words go far deeper than simply recovering wives, children, and possessions, although those things were very important to everyone involved. I'm of the mind that God was speaking specifically to David about recovering the thing he was most in need of in order to fulfill his destiny, HIS FAITH! There was a reclamation project taking place that day and it was his right standing with God! He reclaimed what the devil through doubt and fear had stolen from him sixteen months ago! He defeated more than the Amalekites that day, he defeated the demons that drove him into the arms of the Philistines! Maybe you're trying to hold on to Ziklag while it's being burned to the ground. Leave that place and get back to where God has called you to be and "Recover All!"

Three Things to Remember

1. There's no future in going backwards. An allegiance with the enemy will always fail to deliver the rewards it promises.
2. A gift from the enemy can never yield permanent satisfaction. The world's peace is no substitute for the peace of God which surpasses all understanding.
3. God will always make a way of escape even from the trouble we get ourselves into. God will sometimes use drastic measures to bring us back to where we belong.

Chapter Six
"A lesson on Knowing Your True Identity"

I would like to take some time to look into the lives of four individuals mentioned prominently in the Book of Daniel. Their names are the prophet Daniel himself, and his three friends Hananiah, Mishael, and Azariah. You're probably more familiar with the names Shadrach, Meshach, and Abednego that they were given by the Babylonians. Some may say, what's in a name? My answer would be, probably a lot more than you think!

Let's examine the names and see how they impacted the direction of their lives. First of all there is Daniel whose name means, "God is my judge" the Babylonians named him Belteshazzar which means, "Bel, protect his life," or "Lord of the straitened's treasure." (Which would translate to, "the head of the treasure that belongs to those who are in difficulties.") Simply put Daniel was being assigned to watch over the Hebrew's treasure because they had been brought into captivity. Or Belshazzar which means, "Bel, protect the king." Then we have Hananiah whose name means, "Jehovah is gracious or gift of the Lord" the Babylonians named him Shadrach which means "A tender breast or decree of moon-god." Next there was Mishael whose name means, "Who is what God is?" the Babylonians name him Meshach which means, "expeditious, biting, waters of quiet." Lastly there was Azariah whose name means, "Helped of the Lord or Jehovah has helped" the Babylonians named him Abednego which means, "Servant or worshiper of Nebo or servant of light or sun, worshiper of Mercury or the servant of Jupiter."

It's clear to see the Babylonians had designs on changing the identity of these young men but they were determined to be who God said they were. I'm convinced that during their private times together they never referred to each other by the names given to them by the Babylonians. In holding fast to their God-given names they were taking a stand against anything that would threaten to compromise their convictions. The veracity of that statement is proven by the actions they took when their faith came under attack.

The first incident in which their identity was challenged happened when they were asked to change their diet. For Daniel and his friends Hananiah, Mishael, and Azariah, their dietary habits were a representation of their faith and culture, neither of which they were willing to surrender. In Mosaic Law, God spoke specifically to the Jews about what was clean and unclean as it related to their food intake. The fact they

refused to give in to the Babylonian's
pressure to conform spoke volumes about
their determination to maintain their
identity!

In Daniel 1:11-20 the bible says, So Daniel
said to the steward whom the chief of the
eunuchs had set over Daniel, Hannaniah,
Mishael, and Azariah, "Please test your
servants for ten days, and let them give us
vegetables to eat and water to drink. Then
let our appearance be examined before
you, and the appearance of the young men
who eat the portion of the king's delicacies;
and as you see fit, so deal with your
servants." So he consented with them in
this matter, and tested them ten days. And
at the end of ten days their features
appeared better and fatter in flesh than all
the young men who ate the portion of the
king's delicacies. Thus the steward took
away their portion of delicacies and the
wine that they were to drink, and gave
them vegetables. As for these four young

men, God gave them knowledge and skill in all literature and wisdom; and Daniel had understanding in all visions and dreams. Now at the end of the days, when the king had said that they should be brought in, the chief of the eunuchs brought them before Nebuchadnezzar. Then the king interviewed them, and among them all none was found like Daniel, Hannaniah, Mishael, and Azariah; therefore they served before the king. And in all matters of wisdom and understanding about which the king examined them, he found them ten times better than all the magicians and astrologers who were in his realm.

I don't think it's too much of a stretch to suggest that the child of God's identity is constantly being threatened. In the world today there is a crime which we're all familiar with called "Identity Theft." In fact many people reading this book have possibly been victimized at some time. The damage done by this act occurs when someone gains access to one's personal information and uses it to misrepresent that person, typically in financial matters. It allows the perpetrator to make purchases that are inconsistent with the victim's habits or character thereby doing harm to their reputation. When someone is allowed to steal your identity it gives them the ability to attach your name to their behavior. In the end the victim must use every resource available to track all of the erroneous purchases and work to restore their credibility with the institutions and individuals affected and repair their own image or identity.

Of course as a child of God we must learn to see not only through the natural eye but through the eye of the Spirit. Ephesians 6:12 says, "For we do not wrestle against flesh and blood, but against principalities, against powers, against the rulers of the darkness of this age, against spiritual hosts of wickedness in the heavenly places." Our battle is not in the natural realm but it's in the spiritual realm where we must be prepared to fight. For Daniel, Hananiah, Mishael, and Azariah, the name changes as well as the attempt to change their diet, was seen as a subtle attack from the enemy with the ultimate goal of stealing their identities. They were chosen along with other young men to be proselytized into Babylonian culture and community. The Babylonians would've had them forsake Israel and prefer the Chaldean (Babylonian) lifestyle. But because these young men knew that their identity was inextricably tied to their God and country they refused to cave under the pressure.

How about you and I? Are we convinced that we belong to God? Are we sure of who we are and what our rights and privileges are as God's children? The bible says in Colossians 3:2-3, "Set your mind on things above, not on things on the earth. For you died, and your life is hidden in Christ with

God." When we know who we are our life decisions will be consistent with that knowledge. We must be careful to not allow habits and behaviors that open the door for the devil to steal our identity and misrepresent us to the world. Habits like smoking, drinking, partying, and profanity just to name a few, can be used by the enemy to perpetrate identity theft on the Christian and cause them to live a life that's inconsistent with their confession of faith. When that happens our witness is rendered ineffective and we're incapable of fulfilling the "Great Commission" (Matt. 28:19-20) which every believer is responsible for.

Even when we're victorious against the enemies attack it doesn't mean he won't try again. When Jesus defeated Satan in Luke chapter 4 the bible tells us in verse 13, "Now when the devil had ended every temptation, he departed from Him until an opportune time." It appears that the enemy doesn't give up after a singular defeat, but will resurface later when an opportunity arises. Daniel's friends discovered this to be true when their identities were once again challenged in chapter 3 when they encountered the image of gold. In the book of Daniel chapter 3, King Nebuchadnezzar erects a golden image and gives command to everyone living in the province of Babylon that they would be required to bow down and worship the image whenever instructed to do so. The law stated that at various times music would be played and all peoples, nations, and languages, would be expected to bow down and pay homage to the golden image. The penalty for failing to do so was for those guilty of disobedience to be thrown into a fiery furnace and burned to death.

The three Hebrew boys, Hannaniah, Mishael, and Azariah, or Shadrach, Meshach, and Abednego if you prefer, had made up their minds that they would under no circumstances adhere to this law. They risked their lives to prove their citizenship was in heaven and not Babylon, and that their allegiance was to God over everything and everyone, even King Nebuchadnezzar! Had they accepted their new names and embraced the Chaldean way, bowing down to the image wouldn't have been a problem. They could've just gone along with the crowd and avoided trouble. But there are times when taking a stand for who you are as a child of God will make trouble unavoidable. Daniel 3:8 says, "Therefore at that time certain Chaldeans came forward and accused the Jews." (Meaning they accused Daniel's friends of not bowing down to the image.) After being interrogated by King Nebuchadnezzar they admit to refusing to bow to his image and are consequently thrown into the fiery furnace to die for their crime. I love the statement they make in verses 17-18, "our God whom we serve is able to deliver us from the burning fiery furnace, and He will deliver us from your hand, O king. But if not, let it be known to you, O king, that we do not serve your gods, nor will we worship the gold image which you have set up." How far would you go to protect your identity as a child of God? I think we'd all like to believe we would've stood with them but the truth is many of us would've just bowed down to avoid the fire.

What happens next is one of the great and memorable miracles recorded in scripture. The King was so angry that he instructed that the furnace be heated seven times hotter than what it would normally be. Previously in chapter one the King interviewed them and found them to be ten times better than all of his magicians and astrologers. So I guess if you're ten times better, you can handle seven times hotter! The bible says that when the three boys were thrown into the furnace that a fourth person was seen in the fire with them and that his form was like the Son of God. (3:25) It says in verse 27 they came out of the fire unscathed. In fact, it says the fire had no power over them, the hair of the head wasn't singed, nor were their clothes burned, and the smell of fire was not on them. When you stand for Jesus your faith will protect from the enemies fire!

When it was all said and done not only did they protect their own identities by choosing to stand for God. King Nebuchadnezzar chose to stand with God also after witnessing the power of God in their lives. Daniel and his friends are a tremendous example of what it takes to maintain our identity in a crooked and perverse world. In chapter six we see Daniel also challenged to take a stand and face the Lion's den rather than compromise his identity. He too was protected by his faith in God. God quenched the heat of the fire for Shadrach, Meshach, and Abednego, He shut the mouths of the Lions for Daniel. The good news is He'll do the same for you and me when we take a stand for Him and maintain our identity as a Christian.

How is the world trying to change your identity? What does the enemy say about you? Maybe he calls you an addict, or a gangster, or a cheater, a womanizer, a failure, a liar, unloved, un-forgiven, unwanted, a person with no hope for the future. I say be who God says you are! You are the head and not the tail! (Deut. 28:13) You are more than a conqueror! (Romans 8:37) You are the apple of His eye! (Zechariah 2:8) You are a child of God! (John 1:12) You are His workmanship! (Ephesians 2:10) Are you getting the picture? Don't allow the devil to steal your identity! Be who God says you are in His word because that my friend is your true identity!

Three Things to Remember

1. The fight to maintain our identity will often involve things that seem small and insignificant. Never ignore the conviction of the Holy Spirit.
2. What we see as standing with Christ the world perceives as an attack on their values and beliefs. Don't be afraid of seven times hotter remember you're ten times better.
3. Know who you are in Christ and do everything in your power to be that person. Don't be victimized by the identity thief! "The thief does not come except to steal," John 10:10

Chapter Seven
"A Lesson on God's Selection Process"

I imagine if one researched this particular subject there would likely be an endless supply of opinions about how God chooses the people He desires to use. I wouldn't dare make claims of being an expert, or to possess the ultimate truth beyond all truths. But I do believe I can shed some light on this subject and perhaps share something of value for those who struggle in this area. I know that in the ministry I belong to, that being Victory Outreach, we are constantly reminded that God has chosen or called us. I also know that the great majority of our members have come out of lifestyles that involved drugs, gangs, crime and other degradations that can make the idea of being chosen by God difficult to receive.

With that being said I would draw our attention to a message we traditionally hear about on Palm Sunday. It is most commonly referred to as Jesus' Triumphal Entry into Jerusalem. It fulfilled the prophecy found in Zechariah 9:9 and is recorded in all four gospels. Matthew 21:1-9; Mark 11:1-11; Luke 19:28-44; and John 12:12-19. These passages tell the story of Jesus entering Jerusalem for the final time in the last week of His earthly life. He rides into town on a colt or donkey amidst a great celebration in which the people throw their clothes on the road and wave palm branches (John 12:13), hence the name Palm Sunday. It also marks the start of what we refer to as "Holy Week" beginning on Palm Sunday, continuing through Good Friday, and culminating on Easter or Resurrection Sunday.

There are several aspects of what took place that day that are of significance to me as it relates to how God chooses people. Let's first look at what the bible says in Luke 19:28-36, (When He had said this, He went on ahead, going up to Jerusalem. And it came to pass, when He drew near Bethpage and Bethany, at the mountain called Olivet, that He sent two of His disciples, saying, "Go into the village opposite you, where as you will find a colt tied, on which no one has ever sat. Loose it and bring it here. And if anyone asks you, 'Why are you loosing it?' thus you shall say to him, 'Because the Lord has need of it.'" So those who were sent went their way and found it just as He had said to them. But as they were loosing the colt, the owners of it said to them, "Why are you loosing the colt?" And they said, "The Lord has need of him." Then they brought him to Jesus. And they threw their own clothes on the colt, and they set Jesus on him. And as He went, many spread their clothes on the road.)

First of all, let me just mention that I love when the bible says He went UP to Jerusalem. This doesn't really have anything to do with God's selection process but I can't help but appreciate how everyone who goes to Jerusalem is always going UP! No one in the bible is ever said to have gone DOWN to Jerusalem. It's not a matter of geography it's a matter of spirituality. Whenever we go to the city of God or the house of God, or anyplace where the presence and purpose of God can be found, we are going UP and not DOWN!

But getting back to the point let's look at where the disciples were told to go in order to find what the Lord intended to use for His divine purpose. It was in "the village opposite you," that they were told they would find this colt or donkey if you prefer. The original King James Version uses the word "against" which comes from the Greek word *katenanti-kat-en-an-tee* which basically means directly opposite, which makes the NKJV choice of the word opposite an appropriate selection. A synonym for the word opposite is the word, oppose, which can mean diametrically different.

So the message here is that Jesus asked them to go into a village where the people were not on their side. He sent them to find what He needed in an opposite or opposing village. I would venture to say that many of us were living a life that was diametrically different than the one we're now living. That tells me it's in the ghettos and the inner cities often times where the Lord is looking for people He can use. The bible says in I Corinthians 1:27 that "God has chosen the foolish things of the world to put to shame the wise…" It would've been easier had Jesus said "Go into a village where everyone is on our side…" but most often God never send us the down the easy road. Sometimes the people God chooses to use come from the most unlikely places.

In Jeremiah chapter 38 the prophet finds himself imprisoned in a dungeon. The bible says that in the dungeon there was no water but only mire. It's also said that there was no bread in the city so Jeremiah was destined to sink in the mire and die or starve to death. But God chose an Ethiopian Eunuch named Ebedmelech to rescue Jeremiah. Ebedmelech basically means servant of the king, or slave of the king. What I find interesting in this story is when Ebedmelech asked King Zedekiah for permission to get Jeremiah out of the prison he was first given thirty men to protect him. That speaks to me of God sending His angels to watch over us when we're doing His work. But he then went under the Kings treasury to find something he could use to help Jeremiah. Maybe it's just me but if I'm looking for something of value wouldn't I go in the treasury and not under it? What Ebedmelech did find was old clothes and old rags and they were used to put under Jeremiahs armpits so he could be pulled from the dungeon without harm. If you're a member of Victory Outreach and reading this it should sound like "Treasures Out of Darkness" I mean under the treasury? Old clothes and old rags? It sounds like so many people who were found in the opposite village and appeared to the world to be without value. But God chose us knowing He could mold us into the people we are today.

Another noteworthy phrase is" the colt on which no man has sat." This is a miracle that many believers miss in this narrative. First let me say I'm no animal expert but I've watched my fair share of Animal Planet, Nat Geo Wild or Discovery Channel and learned some facts about nature. One thing I do know is every animal that man uses for transportation, whether it's an Elephant, Horse, Donkey, or Camel, they must be broken before one should expect to ride them without difficulty. It is quite common for the initial experience to include bucking, kicking, and anything else that animal can do in an effort to get the rider off their back. Certainly Jesus being God in the flesh and the creator of all things would be fully aware of the challenges of riding a colt on which no man has sat. This colt or donkey is truly an unlikely and unqualified candidate for the festivities that were about to take place. It would make sense if it were a trained animal, already broken, already proven to be capable of transporting someone. Perhaps it was to prove Jesus is Lord of all creation that He chose to use that untrained and unbroken animal. And the miracle was that colt never bucked or kicked when Jesus sat on him. He submitted to the will of God and behaved himself as they travelled down the streets of Jerusalem.

When I see this colt I see myself. I see Jesus choosing to use someone with no experience and no training. Someone who like the colt, had never come under authority before. Before coming to Christ I bucked, kicked and done whatever I could to avoid being under authority in my life. I wonder how many of us were the unlikely candidate in the opposite village. Maybe there were people in your life like the owner of the colt who questioned why you were chosen. But just like that colt the Lord had need of you! And the miracle for you and me is when we allowed Jesus the position of Lordship over our lives we didn't buck or kick, we simply submitted to His will. That's how I feel when I read this story. I'm the colt upon which no man has ever sat! Sitting in a village opposite Christ needing someone to loose me from what was holding me. And Jesus sent the Holy Ghost to release me from bondage and He prepared me for service.

   And lastly I'm led to consider not only who God chooses, but why God chooses. The bible tells us about the reaction of the disciples as Jesus entered Jerusalem on this young colt. It wasn't only the twelve disciples who responded, but verse 37 says "the whole multitude of the disciples began to rejoice and praise God with a loud voice for all the mighty works they had seen." In John 12:17 it says that one of those works was the raising of Lazarus from the dead. What I'm saying is we were selected or chosen to worship the Lord! The disciples were shouting "Blessed is the King who comes in the name of the Lord! Peace in heaven and glory in the highest!" What happened is that the people were moved to praise and worship the Lord for all He had done! We are called to declare His mighty works in the presence of an unbelieving world. They worshipped with such power that the Pharisees got angry and told Jesus "Teacher, rebuke Your disciples." Jesus said if they keep silent, "the stones would immediately cry out." And on the day of His death the earth quaked and the rocks split! (Matthew 27:51) So it seems that while the people didn't praise or worship Jesus for what He had done, the rocks did!

The fact that many people threw their clothes on the colt for Jesus to sit on and on the road for Him to ride on, speaks of the call to sacrifice. I see God's people putting Jesus over their possessions. Their clothes represented what belonged to them and they were willing to make Jesus Lord over their possessions or substance. By allowing the colt to walk on their clothes, it paints a picture of a people who also submit to who God chooses. I believe worship and sacrifice go hand in hand. A believer shouldn't have one without the other. The bottom line is that we've all been chosen to worship God with our voices, and live a sacrificial life that worships Him with our actions. So no matter where you're from or who you are,

know that you've been selected by God for
His divine purpose!

Three Things to Remember

1. If you see yourself as coming from an opposite village rejoice, Jesus sent His Spirit to bring you out! The fact that you were diametrically different brings God glory.
2. If you see yourself as the colt on which no man has sat rejoice, a miracle was done to bring you into submission.
   Your lack of experience and qualifications will keep you dependant on Christ in every situation.
3. Be a person who's not ashamed to worship in His presence! Live a sacrificial life that brings honor and glory to His name. Because if you don't the rocks will!

Chapter Eight
A Lesson on Laboring in Obscurity

It's possible that you may view the lessons in the previous chapters as only pertaining to those who are called to front line ministry as in preaching, teaching, etc. But I do want to speak to those who do great things for God without getting recognition. There are millions of Christians all over the world who've made a tremendous impact in ministry and we may never know their names because they labor in obscurity. Not everyone has the personality to handle such a role. In most cases if an individual's accomplishments aren't celebrated they may leave that church looking for a place where they'll feel appreciated for their work. That's not necessarily a bad thing. As leaders we should as much as possible recognize publicly the labor of those who work behind the scenes because without volunteerism a church cannot be successful.

But there are those rare people who can serve in ministry through prayer, witnessing, hospitality, giving, and just helping out wherever the need is without ever receiving publicity and still be happy. Most often they are very humble individuals who are uncomfortable with being openly recognized and prefer to trust God for their rewards. People of this caliber are truly one in a million. If a Pastor is fortunate enough to have someone in their congregation with these qualities, they are blessed indeed and generally show their appreciation privately as a means of encouragement for all that they do.

There are a couple of women in the Old Testament who made a monumental contribution to God's work and most Christians are unaware of who they are or what they've done. They show up in Exodus chapter one and their names are Shiphrah which means to be bright; prolific; to procreate, and Puah which means splendor;

light; child bearing; or joy of the parents. They were two Egyptian women who played a significant role in history and are rarely ever mentioned. Their faith and commitment to do what was right make them a tremendous example of how to be happy laboring in obscurity. It also shows that obscurity is only applicable in the eyes of man because with God nothing is obscure. And based on the meaning of their names they were the perfect people for what God had in mind. An act of faith, no matter how small will never go unrecognized by God!

In Exodus 1:15-22 we're given a picture of what type of character these two women had. The bible says, "Then the king of Egypt spoke to the Hebrew midwives, of whom the name of one was Shiphrah, and the name of the other Puah; and he said, 'When you do the duties of a midwife for the Hebrew women, and see them on the birthstools, if it is a son, then you shall kill him;

but if it is a daughter, then she shall live.' But the midwives feared God, and did not do as the king of Egypt commanded them, but saved the male children alive. So the king of Egypt called for the midwives and said to them, 'Why have you done this thing, and saved the male children alive?' And the midwives said to Pharaoh, 'Because the Hebrew women are not like the Egyptian women; for they are lively and give birth before the midwives come to them.' Therefore God dealt well with the midwives, and the people multiplied and grew very mighty. And so it was, because the midwives feared God, that He provided households for them. So Pharaoh commanded all his people, saying, 'Every son who is born you shall cast into the river, and every daughter you shall save alive.'"

Shiphrah and Puah were employed by the Egyptian government to serve as midwives for the Hebrew slaves in Egypt. They were Egyptians themselves and therefore obligated to obey the Pharaoh or king of Egypt. In Exodus 1:8-9 we're told that the new king had no recollection of Joseph or his contribution to Egypt and began to fear the rapid increase of the Hebrews. His fear is that they will outnumber the Egyptians and ultimately rebel and take over the country. In verses 10-14 we see the failure of his initial strategy to slow down the growth of God's people by afflicting them with hard labor. His plan proved to be futile as throughout history we've seen that every attempt to stop the growth and progress of God's people has failed. In Acts chapter 8 the persecution of the church resulted in the promulgation of the gospel into Samaria and Judea.

As the Pharaoh realizes his plan is ineffective he devises a new strategy that involves the genocide of all the male children born to Hebrew women. When the king of Egypt speaks to the women who are employed to function as midwives,

Shiphrah and Puah were the only ones who chose to disobey orders. The bible says in verse 17 that they "feared God" which tells me that even though they were Egyptian the conviction of God was in their hearts. I would imagine that after working with the Hebrew women they had been told about Jehovah God and faith was birthed inside of them. The bible says in Romans 10:17, "So then faith comes by hearing, and hearing by the word of God." Clearly someone had been preaching to these women!

In Matthew 2:16-18 we see a similar action taken by Herod in an effort kill Jesus Christ the savior and Pharaoh's action was an attempt by the devil to prevent the birth of Moses, also a savior. In large part because of the faith and bravery of Shiphrah and Puah Moses was born. Their refusal to participate in genocide, allowed Jochebed, (the mother of Moses) to birth a son, and not see him murdered. They risked their lives because of their convictions. Of course they couldn't have known whose life they were protecting but God did.

It's so awesome to see God's hand in history and how He moves on behalf of those who will take a stand for Him. To disobey a direct order from the Pharaoh was to risk one's life. Their deed didn't go unnoticed. In verse 18 they're asked by the king of Egypt (Pharaoh) "Why have you done this thing, and saved the male children alive?" The explanation they give about the difference between Egyptian women and Hebrew women hardly seems like a valid excuse yet somehow it gets them off the hook. One would've expected the Pharaoh to command they be executed immediately for not following orders. Instead the bible says God dealt well with them. It even goes so far as to say that because they feared God, He provided households for them. (Verse 21) How amazing is that? They disobey Pharaoh and end up getting blessed with houses!

Moses parents, Amram and Jochebed, had to put their child in the river when he was three months old, but had it not been for Shiphrah and Puah, he may never have reached three months. While most people don't know these women God made sure the writer of Exodus included their names because no good deed goes unnoticed by Him. They may be obscure characters to us but certainly not to God! They saved a child God wouldn't use until eighty years later. So they never got a chance to see the fruit of their labor. In all likely-hood these women were long gone by the time Moses began to fulfill the purpose God had called him to.

Thank God for the conviction the Holy Spirit puts in our hearts to steer us away from the path of evil. Our conviction is what's similar to a moral compass. A compass is designed to point north. The idea is that if you're lost, the compass, by showing you which way is north, makes it easy to figure out which way is East, West, or South. In a similar way conviction will point us north or up, if you will. If one stays in tune with God their moral compass should function as a safe guard against sin. Clearly the fact that Shiphrah and Puah "feared" or respected God represented the key to their moral compass. Being a person with strong morals is a good thing but at the end of the day it's holiness that God requires of us.

So if you work in the children's ministry and receive very little recognition take heart, you could be teaching a future Pastor or Evangelist, or Missionary. Perhaps you're an usher or greeter who feels that the work you do doesn't make a difference because it isn't often celebrated. The smile and pleasant attitude you bring may have encouraged hundreds of people who came to church in despair. Sometimes the smallest gesture can have the greatest impact. Even doing security or working the parking lot can make a huge difference for someone. The job you do in security may help the elderly saints who in their golden years simply need to know that they're being protected. Intercessory prayer teams who don't get a lot of credit have prevented countless demons from interfering with the move of God's Spirit during church. Not to mention the protection they provide for the man of God and his family. The bottom line is worth repeating, "No good deed goes unnoticed by God!" Because our God is omniscient, omnipotent, and omnipresent, there is no such thing as obscurity with Him. He sees all and knows all! And He rewards our labors accordingly.

Maybe today like Shiphrah and Puah, the Lord has brought you to a place of decision. Possibly the world and its pleasures are trying to seduce you and lure you into a trap but you hear the voice of God calling you to a higher place. The devil wants you to compromise your convictions but your moral compass is pointing you north. Trust God and do what's right even if no man or woman is there to witness your actions. Take courage and know that His eye is on the sparrow and He watches you also.

Three Things to Remember

1. There are no insignificant acts of obedience to God. Every act of obedience is important to Him. In the realm of the Spirit our obedience is always setting something in motion.
2. There is no authority greater than God's! Even the Pharaoh is subject to His will. It's always right to do the right thing.
3. Shiphrah and Puah's greatest asset was their conviction or moral compass. Make sure your compass is pointing north. Always be obedient to the conviction of the Holy Spirit!

Chapter Nine
A Lesson on Miracles

In order to discuss a miracle it would probably be good to define what a miracle is and what it is not. One dictionary defines it as "a surprising and welcome event that is not explicable by natural or scientific laws and is therefore considered to be the work of a divine agency." Personally, I believe that's about as good a definition as any other. When something happens and it cannot be explained using the laws of nature or science, a divine act has taken place and it should be treated as such. Let me also say this, "God still does miracles today!"

What a miracle is not is something we should routinely expect from God when we though our own poor choices get ourselves into trouble. For example, if you practice bad stewardship over your finances and believe you need God to miraculously provide you with money to cover your shortages it's probably not going to happen. If that's you, unfortunately you don't need a miracle, you need some classes on money management. If you never check the oil on your car or do regular maintenance as a prophylactic and believe you need God to miraculously repair your vehicle whenever it's broken it's probably not going to happen. If that's you, you don't a miracle, you need a mechanic. If you and your spouse don't treat each other right but believe you need God to miraculously give you a good marriage it's probably not going to happen. If that's you, you don't need a miracle, you need a marriage counselor. I think you get the point!

That's not to say that God can't provide for us financially, because He can! It's also not to say He can't fix your car or your marriage, because He can! I'm simply saying we shouldn't expect God to do miracles to cover the bad habits we're making no effort to change. Throughout the bible there are miracles that defied the laws of nature and science. The lame walking, the blind seeing, the mute speaking, the deaf hearing, and the dead being raised all defy the laws of medical science. The plagues of Egypt, the parting of the Red Sea, the parting of the Jordan and many others defy the laws of Nature. It should also be noted that there is in the bible what are called "Penalty Miracles." They are mostly in the Old Testament and include the firstborn children of the Egyptians dying (Exodus 12:29-30), the death of King David's child (II Samuel 12:15-23) and in the New Testament the death of Ananias and Sapphira (Acts 5:1-11). Penalty Miracles were generally performed by God as a punishment for sin.

There exists in the bible a plethora of miracles to choose from. One could make a case for several of them being the subject matter for this discussion. However, the

miracle I would like to focus on occurs in
the third chapter of the book of Acts. It is
primarily discussed in Acts 3:1-10 and it tells
the story of a man who had been lame since
birth being given the power to walk. The
fact that this man is reported to have been
"lame from his mother's womb" (NKJV)
serves to make this story all the more
amazing.

   Acts 3:1-10 says, Now Peter and John
went up together to the temple at the hour
of prayer, the ninth hour. And a certain man
lame from his mother's womb was carried,
whom they laid daily at the gate of the
temple which is called Beautiful, to ask alms
of those who entered the temple; who,
seeing Peter and John about to go into the
temple, asked for alms. And fixing his eyes
on him, with John, Peter said, "Look at us."
So he gave them his attention, expecting to
receive something from them. Then Peter
said, "Silver and gold I do not have, but
what I do have I give you: In the name of

Jesus Christ of Nazareth, rise up and walk." And he took him by the right hand and lifted him up, and immediately his feet and ankle bones received strength. So he, leaping up, stood and walked and entered the temple with them – walking, leaping, and praising God. And all the people saw him walking and praising God. Then they knew that it was he who sat begging at the Beautiful Gate of the temple; and they were filled with wonder and amazement at what had happened to him.

There's so much in these first ten verses that an entire book could be written on just this portion of scripture alone. I do not presuppose that I can exegete every minute detail from this narrative, but I will attempt to expound the revelation God gave me about this particular miracle. First of all, how apropos that this miracle happens in front of the Beautiful Gate at the temple. Of all the places he could've been placed to beg, this seems most appropriate considering how the narrative plays out. When you take into account the man's physical condition clearly he was a prime candidate for something miraculous to take place in his life. Obviously it was an act of God's grace, mercy, and favor of which this man was the beneficiary. God can and will give to whom He desires, when He desires, and owes us no explanation for His choices. But certainly the man in this story has a genuine need. One interesting note is that the writer of the book of Acts (Luke) under the inspiration of the Holy Spirit was not led to include the man's name, only the names of Jesus, Peter and John.

As I consider the life this young man had lived prior to the divine intervention he experienced that day, I can't help but notice how totally dependent he was on the help of others. The bible says he was laid daily in front of the temple at the Beautiful Gate to ask alms or in the common vernacular to beg. His being lame deprived him of mobility and therefore he not only needed help to move but had no control over where he was moved to. It appears that because of his inability to work a regular job and contribute financially to the household, he was assigned the duty of begging as way to help his family. They were certainly aware that his being lame increased his chances of getting sympathy from those who frequented the temple. I don't believe he begged because he wanted to, but because he needed to in order to stay in his family's good grace. That meant that he was not only begging for money, he was also begging for someone to care for him. Imagine living your entire life feeling the need to earn the basic need for love, attention and respect.

The begging would've become like a regular job for him. If he was laid daily at the temple, he would also have been picked up at the end of the day and taken home to turn over the proceeds. Because it had become his job, it also would've become his identity. A carpenter works with wood and their identity is linked to their occupation. A mechanic works on cars and they're identified as one who repairs cars. A beggar begs and is identified as such. He had been begging in front of the temple for so long that practically everyone in town knew who he was and what he did. His identity was simply one of the town beggars. The success he achieved was more dependent upon people's sympathy than their generosity. With all of that being said, it's reasonable to deduce he was not a man of high self-esteem.

Another relevant fact about this young man is that he was outside of the temple. Because of his physical condition he would've only been allowed limited access to the temple. (Leviticus 21:18-23) If we take those things into consideration it's not unlikely that he would've doubted God's love for him as well. Peter and John gave him attention without giving him money. Through the power of the Holy Spirit they discerned that he had a greater need and they were confident that Christ could meet it. When Peter said, "Look at us." The man expected to receive something monetary. In other words he thought it was just an ordinary encounter. But what happened next changed his life forever! When Peter said, "Silver and gold I do not have" I'm sure the young man felt momentarily let down. Suddenly he was given the one thing he needed most but had never been offered to him. Peter allowed the power of Christ to touch through him and instantaneously the man's body was made whole. The words "In the name of Jesus Christ of Nazareth, rise up and walk" had to be the sweetest words he had ever heard.

The bible says "immediately his feet and ankle bones received strength." I love the word "immediately" because it tells me when God is ready to do a miracle He does it without delay. He entered the temple with Peter and John, walking and leaping and praising God. I can imagine the reaction of all those dignified folks in the temple when he began to shake things up with his behavior. There were probably some who wanted him to tone it down a bit. But this was his first day ever to be on his feet and he wanted to experience what everyone mostly takes for granted. He wanted to do all the things he'd only been able to imagine doing prior to his encounter with Christ. I believe he was testing his brand new legs! The ability to walk, jump, dance, and run were all being experienced for the very first time in his life and he was ecstatic! The people recognized him as the town beggar who had been lame and were amazed at what had happened to him.

"A Gait Called Beautiful"

I want to examine the circumstances surrounding this miracle and what I believe contributed to it happening. To view this miracle without seeing the power of Christ manifested through the Holy Spirit would be to miss the most important ingredient. Also to view this miracle without seeing that Peter and John had to meet certain criteria for the Holy Spirit to work through them would be a mistake as well.

It is with a purpose that I used a play on words and inserted the word "Gait" instead of the word "Gate" that occurs in the scripture. I intend to draw our attention to Peter and John and discuss the role they played in bringing about this miracle. The word "Gait" is simply defined as – a person's manner of walking. Like most any minister I desire to see God do miracles through my ministry and in fact I have seen several over the years. But I understand that God needs a clean vessel to move through. In other words, I need to walk right. There are particular aspects of my walk that must be in order if I want to see God use me to work miracles. Because of Peter and John's walk with Jesus they were prepared for the moment. Too many times we are unprepared because of the inconsistency of our walks and therefore lack the faith when the opportunity presents itself.

There are three aspects of Peter and John's spiritual walk that I believe played a significant role in God being able to use them in this capacity. First of all they had **Spiritual Consistency**. They were consistent in their prayer life. There may not be a more important area in which the child of God needs to develop a daily routine. Perhaps the word routine doesn't sit well with you but I only use it in the sense of praying with regularity. The scripture tells us that it was the hour of prayer and as a result Peter and John were going to the temple to pray. Psalm 55:17 says, "Evening and morning and at noon I will pray, and cry aloud, and He shall hear my voice." (NKJV) Evidently this was a pattern to which Peter and John adhered. Some folks behave as though when it's time to pray, it's time to play. They're the ones during prayer service in the foyer talking, or outside fellowshipping, and in some cases on their phones. Peter and John were committed to a lifestyle of prayer and therefore the Spirit of God was able to move through them. If your desire is for God to work miracles through your life, it's imperative that you be consistent in your prayer life.

The other area of consistency I observed with these men is in agreement. Amos 3:3 says, "Can two walk together, unless they are agreed?" It's a rhetorical question to which the answer is no! Not only were these men in agreement about ministering to the lame man but they were also in agreement about who played the lead role and who served in the support role. In my observation I see John's willingness to yield to Peter the lead role and accept his position as a supporter. Their ability to function according to their God given assignments contributed greatly to the success they experienced. Too often in ministry feelings of jealousy, envy, pride, or selfish-ambition can prevent people from operating under God's full anointing. Peter and John were able to put aside those kinds of feelings and focus on glorifying God with their actions and as a result the Lord was able to work miracles through their ministry. What a powerful team they were, Peter preached and John said amen!

They also had **Spiritual Confidence**. I'm in awe of the confidence Peter ministered with. The reward of their commitment to prayer was the confidence to believe God for the impossible. When Peter took the man by the right hand and said, "In the name of Jesus Christ of Nazareth, rise up and walk." He risked being seen as a fake or a phony if the man hadn't been healed. Let's be honest, most of us Pastor's or Minister's would be afraid to make such a bold declaration for fear that God might not come through! It wasn't really their reputation on the line but Gods, and He didn't allow His reputation to be tarnished. Their confidence was in the fact they believed Jesus would do exactly what He said He would. They trusted in the power of the spoken word of God and the lame man was the beneficiary of their faith.

Sometime it's as simple as knowing that God is able! If we are to see God do miracles through our lives then we must not only know He's able, but also that He's willing. They had a confidence that said it's not the size of the task but the size of my God! Our confidence in God's proven ability to come through is critical if we need a miracle. Our faith must grow beyond the place of asking "how" God is able to simply "knowing" He's able. (Perhaps we should echo the Psalmist and say, "If it had not been for the Lord who was on our side," Psalm 124:1 where would we be?) Having that mindset would be a reminder of the miraculous work God has already done in delivering us from our sin. When we say God is able it's not conjecture but it's stating a fact. If our minds and hearts can accept that statement as factual we have the opportunity to walk as Peter and John walked. There's no greater place to put ones confidence than in God's ability to produce miracles.

Lastly, they had **Spiritual Compassion**. The compassion that is born of the Spirit isn't just sympathetic but it's empathic. Sympathy says, "I feel sorry for you." While empathy says, "I feel what you feel." Peter and John were empathic leaders. This attitude is revealed in how they responded to the lame man and his need. When we encounter individuals who are unsaved it helps to remember what it felt like to be estranged from Christ. I believe Peter and John remembered the overwhelming joy they experienced when Jesus was revealed to them. It was because of that characteristic they were compassionate enough to not only pray for him but to walk with him. Spiritual Compassion allows us to walk with those who come to Christ. The man who had previously been lame was now running and leaping and praising God! As he entered the temple with Peter and John his behavior was very unorthodox and disruptive to the religious folks, but they walked with him as he held on to their hands. We need the compassion to walk with new converts and hold their hands during those times when their enthusiasm produces unusual behavior.

Not only did Peter and John walk with him but they also rejoiced with him. This man was overflowing with joy because of the miracle God had done for him. People with Spiritual Compassion don't have a problem rejoicing with others. Compassion will move us beyond envy, jealousy, or selfishness and allow us to celebrate God's blessing on someone else's life. In Acts 4:22 the bible says that the man who received the miracle was over forty years old. The scripture also says in Acts 3:2 that he had been lame from his mother's womb. So this would've been the first time in his life he had ever been on his feet. I'm thinking there was some serious rejoicing going on! His enthusiasm would've been uncontrollable! Sometimes when a person's rejoicing is what we consider "over the top" we tend to distance ourselves from them. But that was not the case for Peter and John. They were happy to be associated with him and share in his joy. What a great place to be in our walk with God! These men truly had a **Beautiful Gait!**

Three Things to Remember

1. A Beautiful Gait is a life that has Spiritual Consistency. Consistent in prayer and agreement with those you co-labor with.
2. A Beautiful Gait is a life that has Spiritual Confidence. Confident enough to put God's reputation to the test and believe that He's able.
3. A Beautiful Gait is a life that has Spiritual Compassion. Compassion to walk with those God heals or saves and to rejoice with them also.

Chapter Ten
"One Final Lesson"

As I strive to be a man of **Destiny &
Courage** or a man who cooperates with
God, I've had to fight many battles along
the way. And the truth be told, I'm still
fighting today to be that man. There have
been and will be many days when like the
Apostle Paul I'm a man whose soul is in
conflict. In Romans 7:13-25 the Apostle
speaks of a constant struggle against sin in
the world and in the inner man or soul. He
says in verse 15, "For what I will to do, that I
do not practice; but what I hate, that I do."
Verse 17 says, "But now, it is no longer I
who do it, but sin that dwells in me." I have
to say that on many occasions that sounds
like my life.

There's no denying it saints, we're in a
life-long battle against sin. I wish I could
share with you some magic formula that
would transform you so that all of your

struggles would disappear and you'd live a sin free life, but the truth is there is no such remedy. But there is power in the name of Jesus! Living a life where prayer, fasting, the word of God, and fellowship with the saints are prioritized will lead to more victories than defeats! In other words, we'll win far more battles than we lose!

I believe the mature Christian is reminded of Romans 8:1-2 that says, "There is therefore now no condemnation to those who are in Christ Jesus, who do not walk according to the flesh, but according to the Spirit. For the law of the Spirit of life in Christ Jesus has made me free from the law of sin and death." Failure may happen even to mature Christians but condemnation need not be the result. We must focus on walking in the Spirit and living a life that's diametrically different than those in the world.

"On Every High Hill and Under Every Green Tree"

In my reading of the Old Testament I've come across this statement on more than one occasion. There are two places in particular I'd like to examine. I Kings 14:22-23 says, "Now Judah did evil in the sight of the Lord, and they provoked Him to jealousy with their sins which they committed, more than all their fathers had done. For they also built for themselves high places, sacred pillars, and wooden images on every high hill and under every green tree." Also in II Kings 17:9-10 the bible says, "Also the children of Israel secretly did against the Lord their God things that were not right, and they built for themselves high places in all their cities, from watchtower to fortified city. They set up for themselves sacred pillars and wooden images on every high hill and under every green tree."

When I consider the phrase "on every high hill and under every green tree" it speaks to me about those in the world and those in the church. The word "high" used in this scripture is taken from the Hebrew word *gabowahh – gaw-bo-ah* which can mean haughty, or prideful. The word "hill" is from the Hebrew word *gibah – ghib-aw* which means hill, or little hill. Or to put it plainly "a proud little hill". The insight God gave me from this speaks about people who think they're bigger or more important than they really are. The hill only thinks it's high because there are no mountains in the vicinity. If it were next to a mountain it would have proper perspective and possibly be less prideful.

In Luke 14:7-11 Jesus teaches about staying humble. The bible says, So He told a parable to those who were invited, when He noted how they chose the best places, saying to them, "When you are invited by anyone to a wedding feast, do not sit down in the best place, lest one more honorable than you be invited by him; and he who invited you and him come and say to you, 'Give place to this man.' And then you begin with shame to take the lowest place. But when you are invited, go and sit down in the lowest place, so that when he who invited you comes he may say to you, 'Friend, go up higher.' Then you will have glory in the presence of those who sit at the table with you. For whoever exalts himself will be humbled, and he who humbles himself will be exalted." So my advice is if you're a hill don't try to make yourself a mountain, let God make you a mountain. Get the picture?

Here's the revelation that the Lord gave me where I see a connection to those in the world. The idea is based on the notion that God sits high and looks low. If God in fact looks down on creation from heaven then anything done a "high hill" would be done in plain sight. In other words this equates to openly sinning with no regard for the judgment of God. This refers to people who don't fear God and therefore see no need for restraint or repentance. They reject the reality of heaven or hell and choose to live their lives on their own terms without any boundaries. To sin on "every high hill" is to be in total rebellion against God and the plan He has for mankind.

We've considered the "high hill" so now let's examine the "green tree". This phrase speaks to me about those in the church who practice sin. The word "green" is taken from the Hebrew word *raanan – rah-aw-nan* which means green, verdant, prosperous-green, or flourishing. So this phrase speaks of a green and flourishing tree. This represents those who appear fruitful and productive but in their private life there is a struggle with sin. They differ from the "high hill" in the fact that they'd never sin openly. They're fully aware that their behavior is unacceptable and so they hide behind their reputation as a Christian or leader. There are several reasons for someone arriving at this place. One of which could be the result of being indoctrinated with a grace heavy theology that can sound as though it excuses sin.

But the bible says in Hebrews 13:8 "Jesus Christ is the same yesterday, today, and forever. Since Jesus Christ is God, we could say God is the same yesterday, today, and forever. That being said, we see God's position and judgment of sin in the Old Testament. If God is the same today then He hates sin now as much as He did then. This is the reason He (Jesus) lives to make intercession for those of us who come to God through Him. (Hebrews 7:25) This also illustrates why the world is desperately in need of our Savior Jesus Christ!

Once again following the train of thought that God sits high and looks low, this refers to those who to the human eye would be unseen. If a man were looking down from an elevated position he couldn't see what's happening under a "green tree". But it's not man's eye that is to be considered, it is God's eye! Because of His omnipresence God is aware of what happens on every high hill and under every green tree. I believe this is worse than the high hill because the green tree is like the fig tree Jesus cursed. The tree appeared from a distance to be fruitful, but upon close examination it was revealed to be unproductive and fraudulent. It was cursed for perpetrating fruitfulness. How much more will there be harsh judgment on the Christian who uses his faith as cover for unrighteousness. Jesus says in John 15:22, "If I had not come and spoken to them, they would have no sin, but now they have no excuse for their sin."

   The bottom line is if you're on the road to maturity you would be wise to avoid either one of these situations. As a person of

Destiny & Courage we will always battle against sin in the world and in ourselves. But thanks be to God who gives us the victory through our Lord Jesus Christ! (I Corinthians 15:57) I'm determined to fulfill my purpose in life as a servant of the Lord and there are many lessons I must yet learn. But I do my best to stay focused on my calling and I work hard at becoming a mature man of God. Someone told me once that growing old is not the same as growing up. Growing old requires no effort on our part, it's a natural process. However growing up doesn't happen without effort! So my prayer is that this book will provide you with some insight that will motivate you to strive for maturity in your **Christian Life.** At the end of the day maturity is part of our **Destiny** and it will take **Courage** to obtain it!

54426843R00081

Made in the USA
San Bernardino, CA
16 October 2017